FUN IN WEST CARIBBEAN

Chelsea Kong

© 2024-2025 Chelsea Kong

All rights reserved. All images used in this book are licensed copies from their respectful owners including Jasmine Kong, Freepik, Ghetty Images, Canva, others. This book or any portion thereof may not be reproduced or used in any manner whatsoever without the express written permission of the publisher except for the use of brief quotations in a book review.

Printed in 2024-2025, Made in Toronto, Canada
ISBN: 978-1-998335-10-7
Hardcover ISBN: 978-1-998335-22-0
Library and Archives Canada

CHELSEA'S

Your dad and mom books a cruise. They need to choose a cruise line. A cruise line is a company that does cruises for different months, weeks, and months in a year to different places.

PROMO

Summer in
West Caribbean

Enjoy summer nights in great weather & fun!

安利遊輪假期
www.traveldesigncruises.com

8 Days 7 Nights — Only **$576 USD** /person

BOOK NOW

+310.803.7050   www.traveldesignusa.com

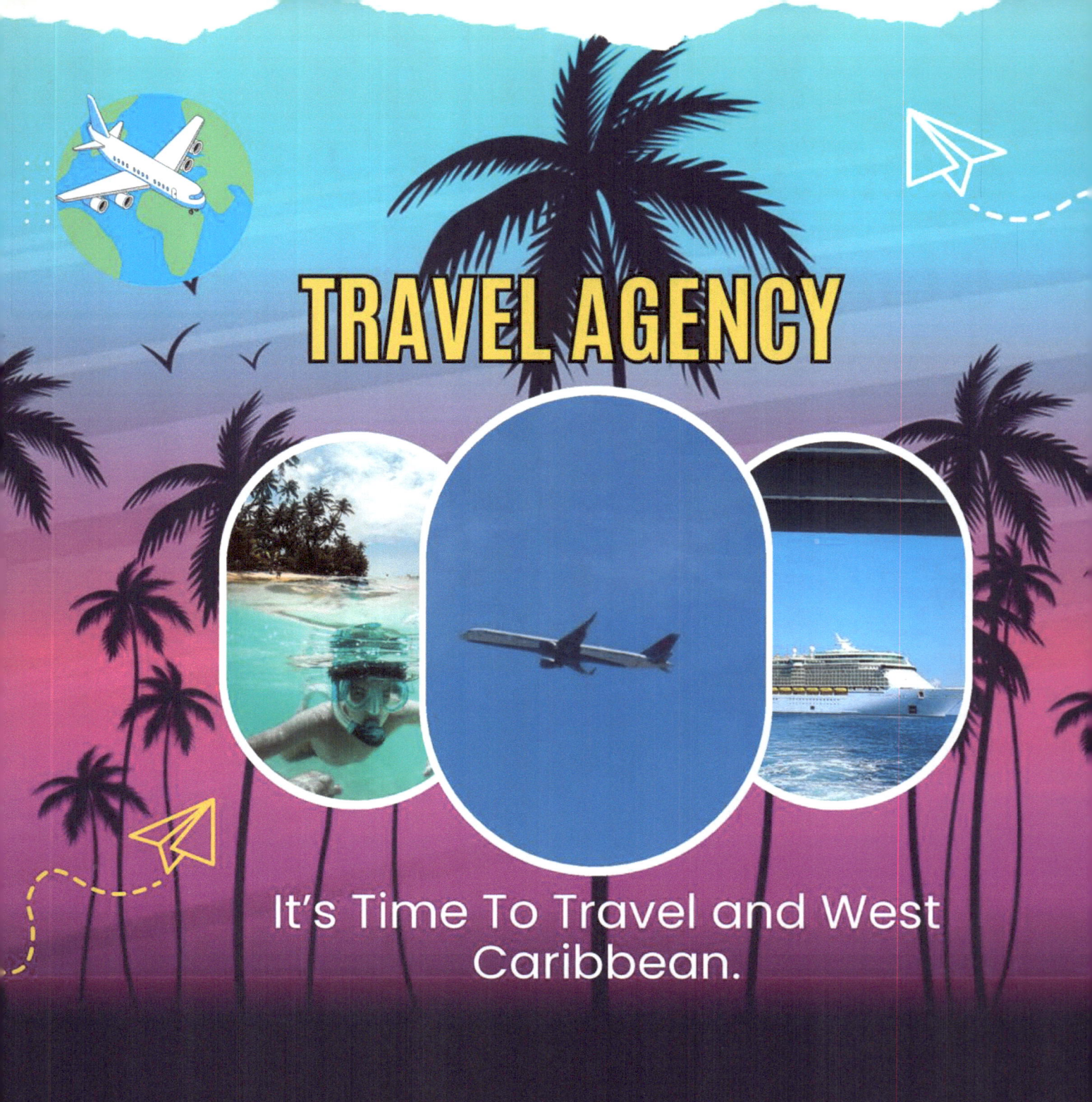

FUN THINGS TO DO

There are lots of fun things to do and places to explore at the different ports. The cruise boat will stop at sea ports. You can get off the boat and have fun.

There are fun things to see and to do in Florida if you arrive one day earlier.

Everglades Airboat ride
Jungle Queen Riverboat
Water Taxi

Coral Beach
Seven Mile Beach
Blowhole and lighthouse

Konoko Falls

Dolphin Cove

Botannical Garden

Dunn's River Falls

Orcho Rios

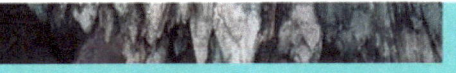
Green Grotto Caves

Falmouth, Jamaica

Nassau, Bahamas

There are important buildings, beautiful island views, forts, Paradise Island Harbour, Queen's Staircase, and dolphins, turtles, sharks, and more.

COCO CAY, BAHAMAS

A private island with a water park for Royal Caribbean tourists.
There are lots of things you can do here.

Rules

1. Be on time
2. Obey your parents
3. Follow directions
4. Listen carefully
5. Be kind

TIME TO BOOK NOW

Flights go on sale.
Your parents need to buy them 5 months earlier to make sure you have good seats.
Flights may be in USD.

FLIGHT SALE

BOOK NOW

Your dad and mom can choose the seats.
Delta Airlines has window and middle seats.
You can collect points to use in the future for free flights.

Check in

Your dad and mom need to check in.
They use the cruise app.
This will keep your cruise vacation.
The room needs to be fully paid.

BOOK NOW

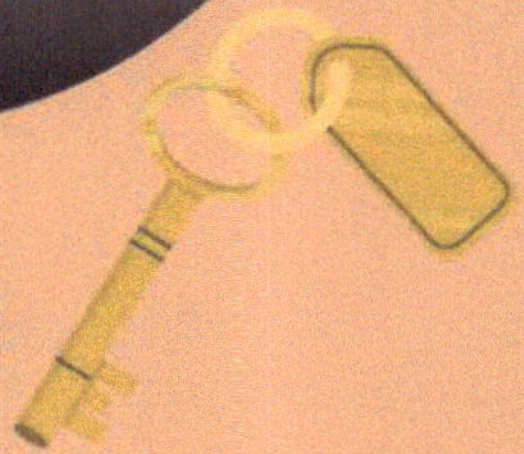

Your parents will look for the best prices for hotel rooms. You will need a place to stay if you go to Florida a day before.

Plan your vacation days well.
You have breakfast and then go places.
Do fun activities in the morning to lunch.

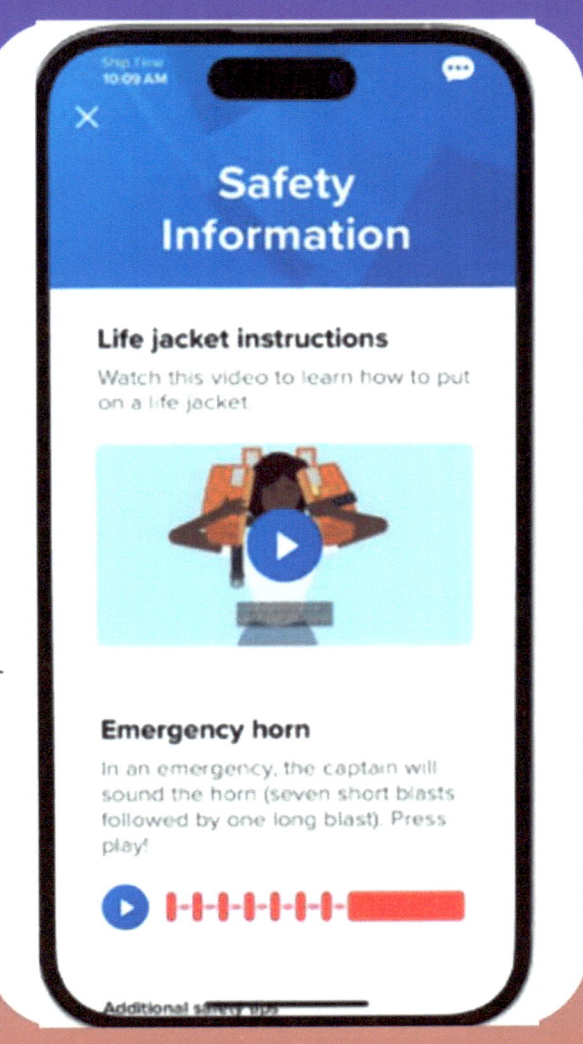

Parents have to check in on the app. It makes the cruise check in faster. There is another check for the cruise.

YOUR AMAZING Travel

Your parents need to plan the rides. They will want a ride to the airport, hotel, and to the seaport.

Your parents will need to help you pack the luggage with everything you need. They need to follow rules of the airport.

Check the weather.
You need to have the right clothes.
You need extra clothes, too.
Ask help from your parents.

REMINDER

Set the alarm before you sleep.
Make sure you packed everything.
You need to be at the airport early.
You need to be there 3 hours ahead.

Time to go to the airport.
You may take a car or a shuttle.

Security Check

Show your passport and boarding pass.
You need to do a screening check.
Take your things.
Go to the gate to wait.

The airplane leaves the airport.
It lands at Ft. Lauderdale Airport.
Get your luggage.
Your parents need to call for the hotel shuttle to go to the hotel.

HOTEL

Take the shuttle to the hotel for free.
Check into the hotel.
You can unpack there.

Travel one day before.
Check restaurants in the area.

Ft. Lauderdale

Everglades National Park
It has many hiking trails in famous mountains. There are guides to help you.

Holiday Lights Boat Tour
This boat tour lets you enjoy exciting things to do like kayaking. You will go to famous rivers and different places.

Airboat Adventure
They have the newest bicycles and you can go to different famous bicycle routes.

Broading the Cruise

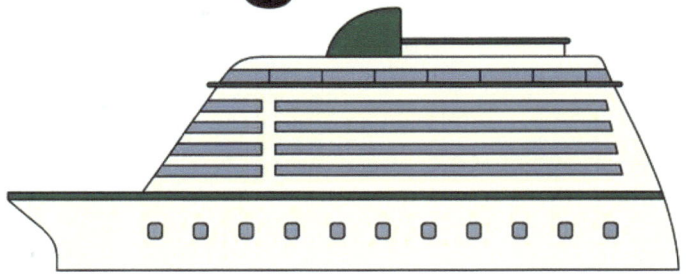

The cruise boat will let people on the boat at 11:30am to 1pm. Somebody will check your family in. After everyone is on board, they will leave.

Check in is faster through the app.
There is a security check.
Then more checks are done.

They will take your bags to your room.
You can go have lunch and have fun.
Your room will be ready after that.

The cruise has three different rooms.
The middle of the ship is the best.
The front and back rooms are cheaper.
The ocean view room is the best.

PICKLEBALL

This is a fun game to play and easy to learn.
Try it and you will see.
A lot of people like to play this game too.
You need to be there early.

SPORTS AND MORE!

There are other sports and things to do on the cruise boat while at sea and in the night.
Your parents will need to book ahead of time.

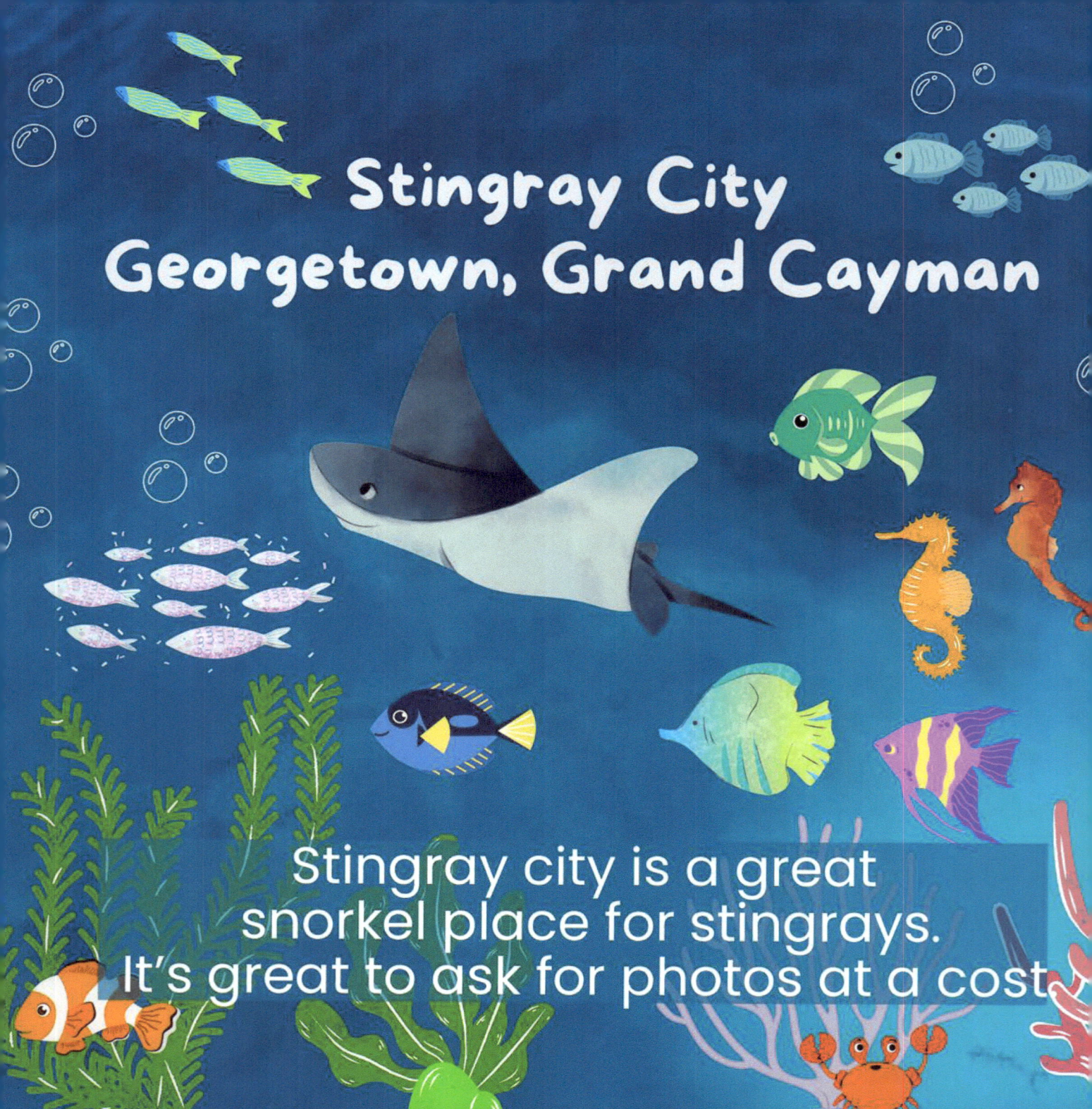

Take photos with the stingray.
Watch out for their tail as they sting.
They swim fast too.

Starfish Point Beach

You can see starfish on this beach. It's a great place to get photos. Keep them in the water.

You can enjoy the sun as you take a walk on Seven Mile Beach.
Take a tour to swim with turtles and dolphins, kite surfing, kayak, paddle boarding sailing, and more.

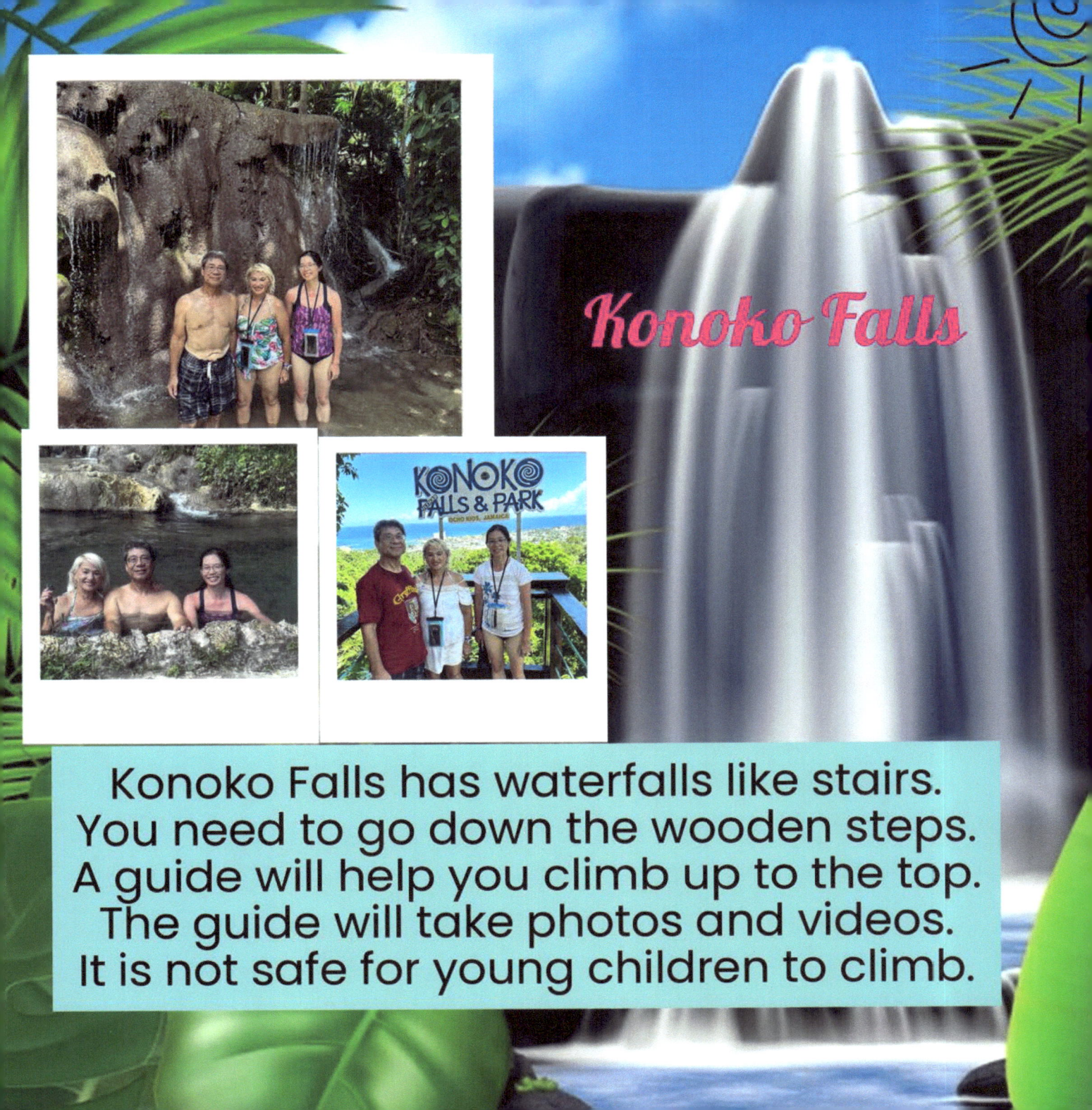

BOTANNICAL GARDEN & ZOO

There is a zoo with different animals.
There are flowers, plants and trees.
It is beautiful to take photos.

DUNN'S FALLS

This is like a large beautiful staircase.
You need a guide to help you climb.
It is not safe for children.

LABADEE, HAITI

Arawak Aqua Park

Labadee Snorkel Safari

Nelly's Beach

These are a few places and things to do.

Bucaneer's Bay

Colubus Cove

Amiga Island

The cruise will cancel this if it's not safe. They will give your parents their money. They will let them book a new activity.

NASSAU, BAHAMAS

Come and see these places:
Bahamas Museum, Rawson Square,
Queen's Staircase

Nassau, Bahamas

Pearl Island Beach Escape
Nassau Sail & Reef Snorkeling
Baha Bay Water Park
Seaworld Explorer
Blue Lagoon Island Shark Encounter
New Providence Sightseeing Tour

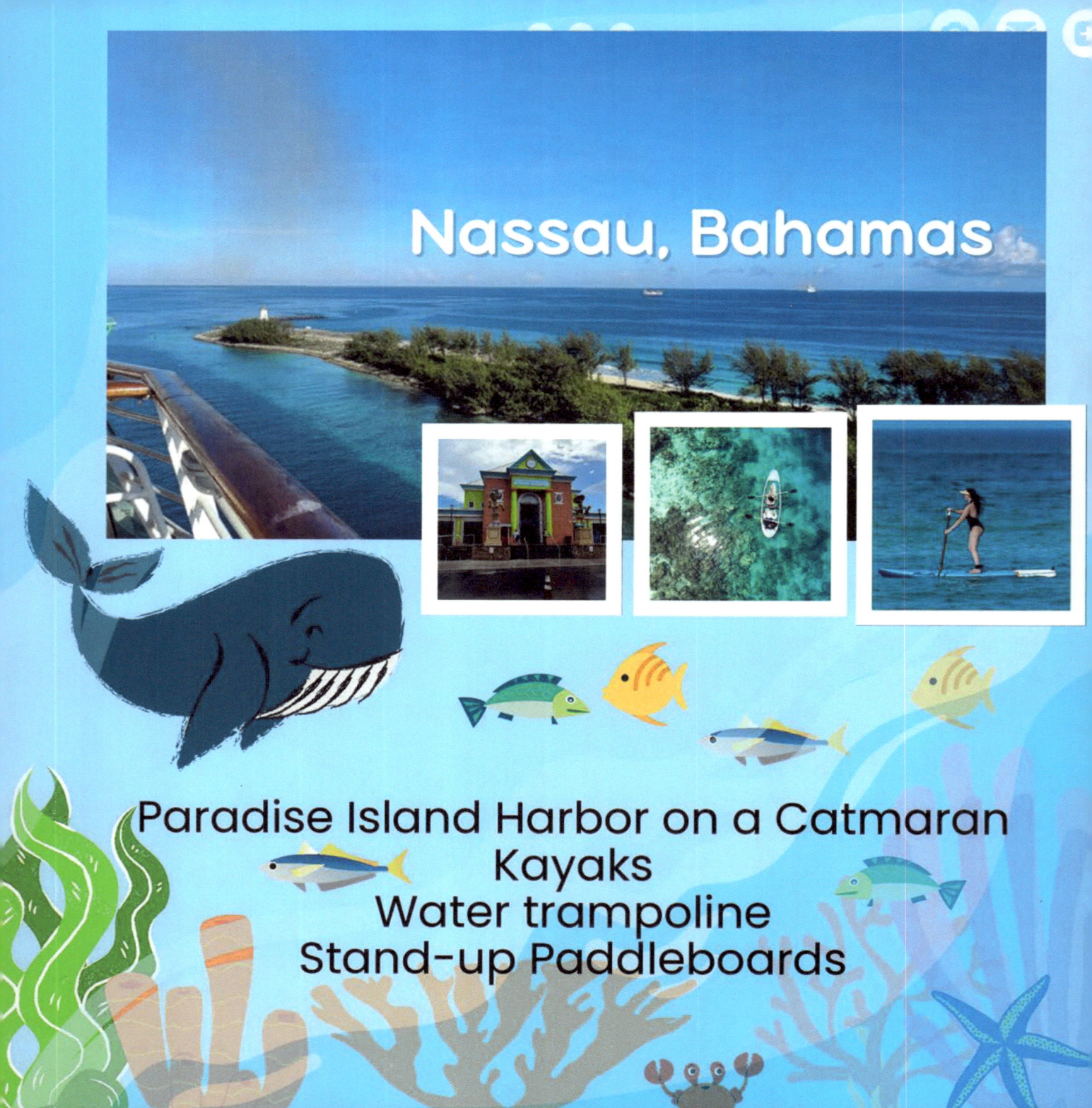

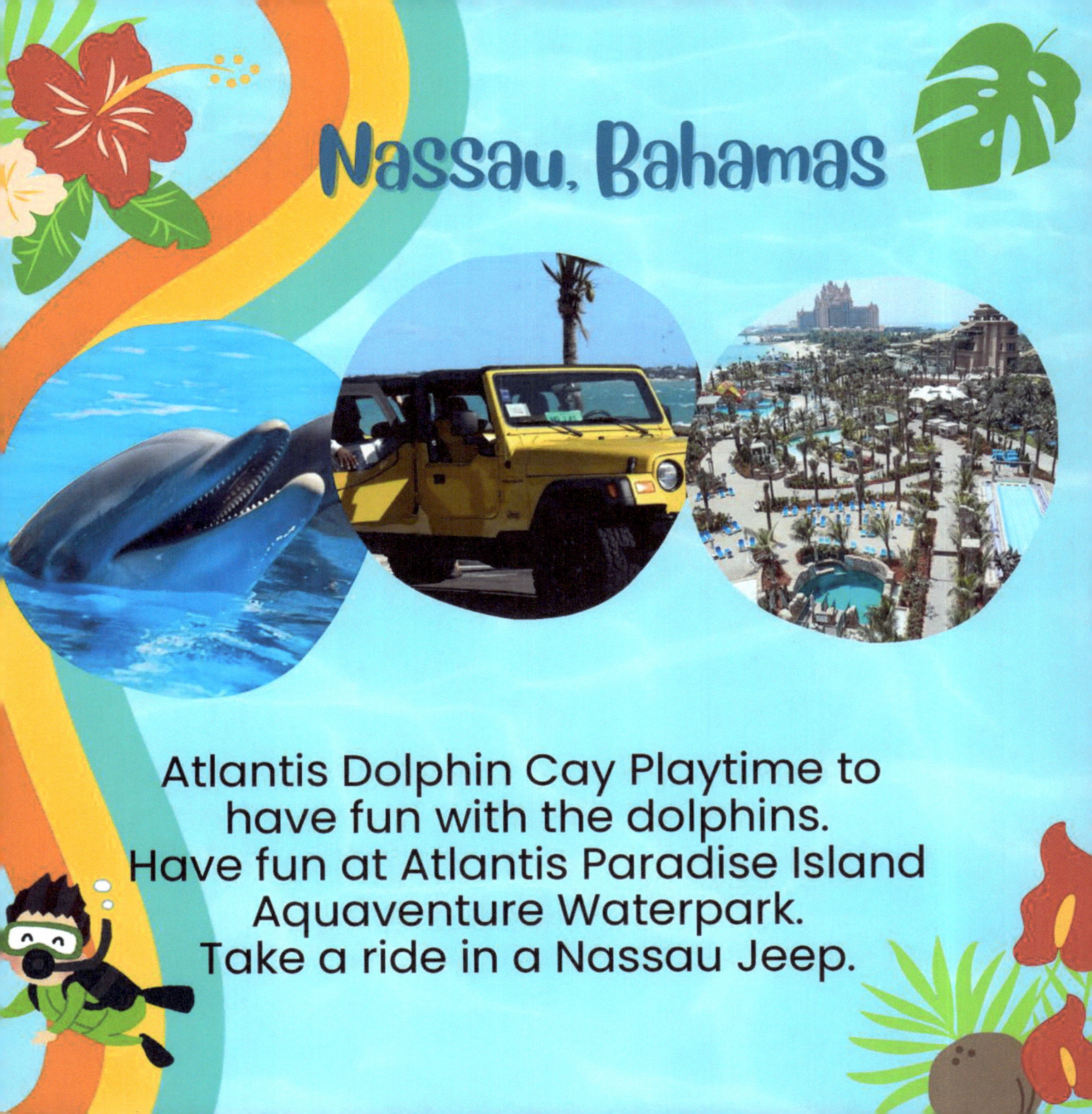

Nassau, Bahamas

Take a visit to Fort Charlotte, Fort Fincastle and Fort Montagu, or a fishing tour.
There are things to do on Harbour Island and Paradise Island.

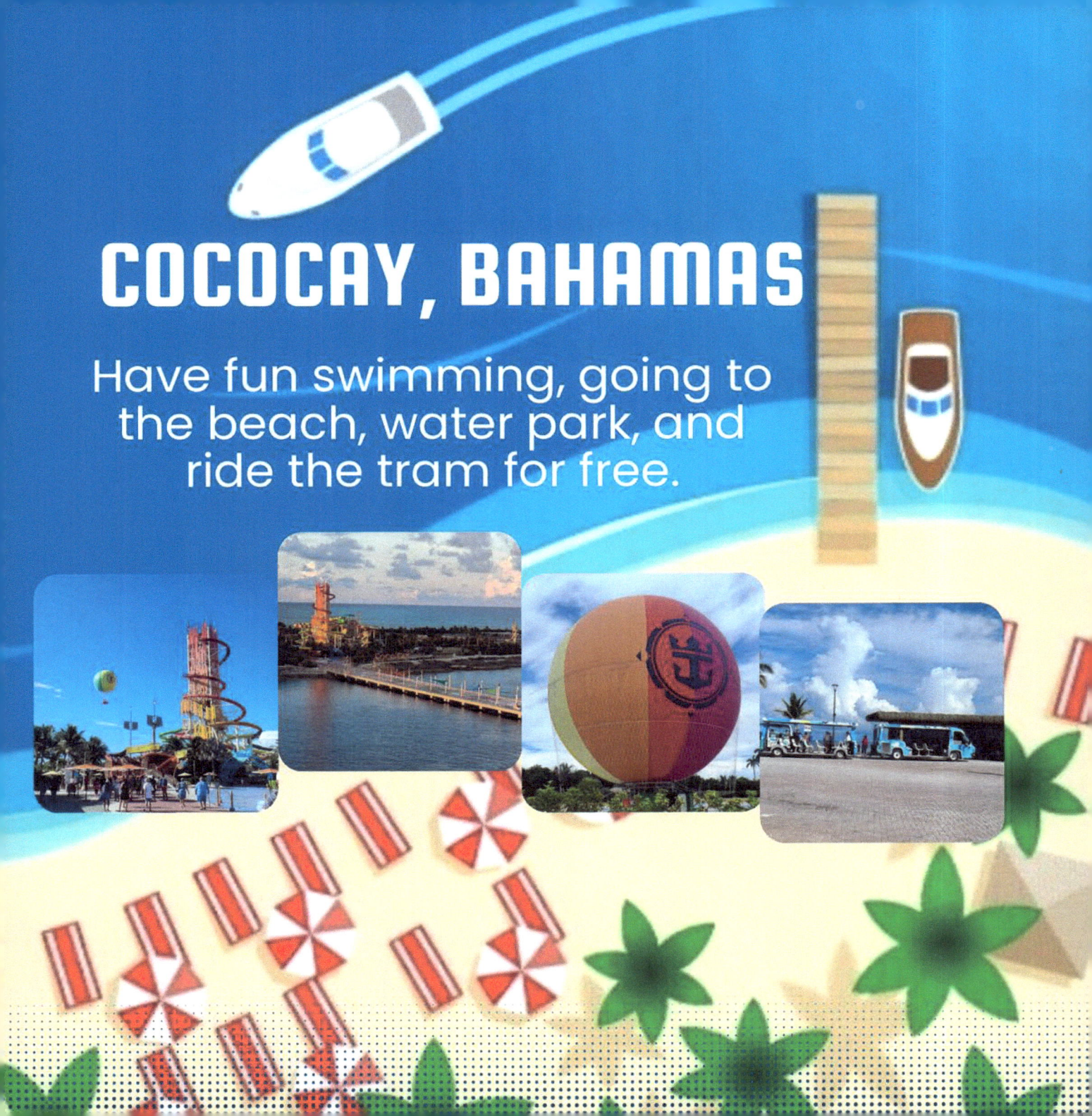

You need walkie talkies on the island.
You need the internet to use the app.
The zipline goes around the island.
There are other sports to play.

COCO CAY, BAHAMAS

Snorkeling
Kayaking
Thrill Water Park
Captain Jill's Galleon

Splash Summit
Splashaway Bay
Wavepool
Chill Island

There are a lot of water sports here.

MORE FREE PLACES

South Beach
Oasis Lagoon
Sports Court
Pickleball

EXPLORE YOUR DESTINATION

CocoCay Photos

Restaurants

These restaurants give free food for cruise guests:
Skipper's Grill
Captain Jack's
Chill Grill
Snack Shack

There are three Snack Shack restaurants.

There are restaurants that you have to pay.
You can do all day snorkeling.
There are free things to do.

Take lots of photos and videos.
Have fun all day!
Go back to the boat before 5pm.

Reminder!

Pack your things the night before. You need to make room for things. Have extra clothes to wear. You won't be able to get anything after. If you don't need them to take your luggage, you can take care of it. You need to bring it with you and leave the room by 9am. They want everyone off the ship by 9:30a.m. on the last morning.

The cruise boat will take you back to Fort Lauderdale Cruise Port.
Take the shuttle to the airport.
You need to arrive 3 hours ahead of time.

You need to check in before the flight.
Then go through the security check.
You need to show the boarding passes.
You will arrive back at your home airport.

Your family needs to get the luggage.
Go through another security check.
Then you can go home.

LIFE CAN BE GREAT IF YOU KNOW HOW TO USE YOUR TIME WELL. REMEMBER FAMILY.

TRAVEL SAFELY

DO WELL IN SCHOOL. PLAN, BE SMART, WORK, SAVE, GIVE, HAVE FUN.

References

Royal Caribbean, "Shore Excursions" Royal Caribbean, 2024.
https://www.royalcaribbean.com/booked/shore-excursions

Visit Florida, "City of Fort Lauderdale" Visit Florida, 2024.
https://www.visitflorida.com/places-to-go/southeast/fort-lauderdale/

Cayman Islands, "Tours & Adventures" Cayman Islands, 2024.
https://www.visitcaymanislands.com/en-us/things-to-do/tours-adventures

References

Royal Caribbean, "George Town, Grand Cayman" Royal Caribbean, 2024. https://www.royalcaribbean.com/cruise-to/george-town-grand-cayman

John Shallo, "Best Things to do in Falmouth, Jamaica" Cruise Addicts, October 29, 2023. https://cruiseaddicts.com/best-things-to-do-in-falmouth-jamaica/

Royal Caribbean, "What to do in Falmouth, Jamaica" Royal Caribbean, June 5, 2020. https://www.royalcaribbean.com/blog/inside-look-what-to-do-in-falmouth-jamaica/

References

Royal Caribbean, "Labadee, Haiti" Royal Caribbean, 2024.
https://www.royalcaribbean.com/cruise-to/labadee-haiti

Royal Caribbean, "Nassau, Bahamas" Royal Caribbean, 2024.
https://www.royalcaribbean.com/cruise-to/nassau-bahamas

Royal Caribbean, "CocoCay Cruises" Royal Caribbean, 2024.
https://www.royalcaribbean.com/cococay-cruises

Message from the Author

Thank you for reading this book. I hope you can leave a good review to encourage me to write more books to teach children and adults. Fun in the West Caribbean is about my vacation to West Caribbean. VIA Rail was part of the plan. It is good to become a VIA Rail preference member if you travel within Canada. You can collect enough points to get free rides. There are places and things to do not included in this book.

OTHER PRODUCTS

- Knowing God
- How to Hear God's Voice
- New Life in Jesus
- Loving Israel
- God's Gifts/Spiritual Talents
- Meeting God
- Word Power
- Fruit of the Spirit
- The Tabernacle
- Bride for Jesus
- A Life of Prayer
- Live Free
- Who am I in Jesus
- Walk in Love
- God's Favor
- Man of God
- Woman of God
- How to Use Money
- God's Wisdom
- Fasting
- See Jerusalem and Bethany
- First Fruit Offering
- Feast of Trumpets
- Day of Atonement
- Feast of Tabernacles
- Counting the Omer
- Festival of Lights
- Glory, Presence, and Holy Spirit
- Live in God's Presence
- Pentecost
- See Galilee, Nazareth, and Tiberias
- Hear God Speak
- Knowing Jesus
- Knowing Holy Spirit
- A Healthy Life and Healthy Life Work Book
- Smokey the Cat
- Passover Unleavened Bread
- Resurrection Life
- The Blessing
- Revival
- Chelsea Learns Hebrew
- Thanksgiving
- Give Thanks
- Jesus Birth
- Loving Jesus: Bride and Groom
- Proverbs 31 Woman

OTHER PRODUCTS

ABC of People in the Bible
Colours in the Bible
Breakthroughs
Open Doors
The Seven Spirits of God
Numbers in the Bible
Aglee the Eagle
An Eagle's Life
Chelsea Learns Numbers in Hebrew
ABC's of Faith
Feast of Purim
A Royal Life
Family Day
Family Blessings
Chinese New Year
Pandas
Worship
Pandas
Canada
Celia's Birthday
Animal Stories
Eagles

Devotionals
31 Day Devotional

Inspirational/Other
Chelsea's Psalms and Poems
Your Daily Meal: Chelsea's Photo Album
Chelsea's Psalms and Poems2
Travel West Caribbean

Puzzle Books
Biblical Puzzle Book Vol 1-5
Bible Puzzles for Young Children Book 1-3
Biblical Puzzle for Children Books 1-5
Chelsea's Bible Puzzles

OTHER PRODUCTS

Teaching Series

How to Hear God's Voice Teaching Guide & Audio Book

Relationship with God, Jesus, Holy Spirit Guide

Knowing God, Jesus, Holy Spirit Guide & Audio Book

Flowing in the Prophetic

Teaching (Non-Sale on my website)

Purim

Passover

Resurrection

BOOK REVIEWS

More books on Amazon, Kobo, and Barnes and Noble, Smashwords, and IngramSpark.
https://chelseak532002550.wordpress.com/

More books on Amazon, Kobo, and Barnes and Noble, Smashwords, and IngramSpark.
https://www.amazon.com/author/chelseakong

Please leave a review and share with friends to help the author continue to write more books to reach more readers. Thank you so much for your support.

Review!

About
CHELSEA KONG

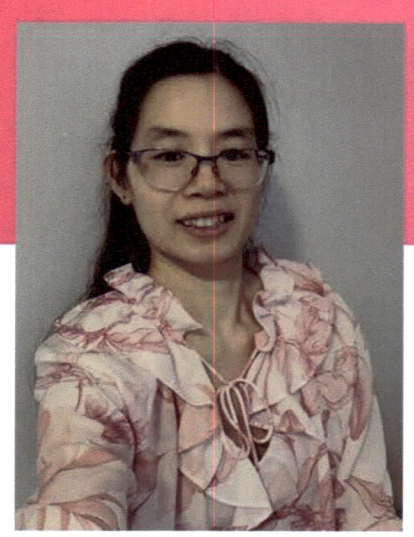

She is a writer, creative arts and digital media artist, skilled administration and certified PCP (Payroll Compliance Professional), and podcaster. Chelsea also served in a variety of roles, from audiovisual, photography, to assisting on the worship team, and ministry team. She also has a passion for families being united.

Chelsea has been a guest on Unity Live Radio, The Lady Tracey Show, and How to Live for Christ and is highly recommended by a Proud Christian blog. She is also a guest blogger. A few of her books have been featured in YourAuthorHub, etc. She graduated from Hotel and Restaurant Management, Digital Media Arts, Office Administration, Payroll Compliance Professional, and experience working with children. Chelsea lives in Toronto, Canada. She mainly writes children's books, stories, bridal writing, poems, lyrics for songs, words of encouragement, blessings, prayers, and jokes. The author of How to Hear the Voice of God, the Bridal Collection, Knowing God, etc. She also has her own Bible Puzzle books and other inspired products. Her podcast channel is called Chelsea K on Anchor, Spotify, and iTunes.

Please check my website to find out more:
https://chelseak532002550.wordpress.com/

www.ingramcontent.com/pod-product-compliance
Lightning Source LLC
Chambersburg PA
CBHW042054050526
44107CB00110B/1149